OnBoard
ACADEMICS

Stories

© 2015 OnBoard Academics, Inc
Portsmouth, NH
800-596-3175
www.onboardacademics.com
ISBN: 978-1-63096-042-1

OnBoard Academic's books are specifically designed to be used as printed workbooks or as on-screen instruction. Each page offers focused exercises and students quickly master topics with enough proficiency to move on to the next level.

OnBoard Academic's lessons are used in over 25,000 classrooms to rave reviews. Our lessons are aligned to the most recent governmental standards and are updated from time to time as standards change. Correlation documents are located on our website. Our lessons are created, edited and evaluated by educators to ensure top quality and real life success.

Interactive lessons for digital whiteboards, mobile devices, and PCs are available at www.onboardacademics.com. These interactive lessons make great additions to our books.

You can always reach us at customerservice@onboardacademics.com.

Story Elements

Key Vocabulary

story element

character

setting

events

problem

solution

The Ant and the Grasshopper

In a field one summer's day, a grasshopper was hopping and singing to its heart's content. An ant passed by, dragging an ear of corn to its colony.

"Why not come and chat with me," said the grasshopper, "instead of toiling in that way?"

"I am helping to store food for the winter," said the ant, "and I recommend that you do the same."

"Why worry about winter?" said the grasshopper. "There is plenty of food." But the ant continued on its way.

When the winter came, the grasshopper had no food and found itself hungry – while it saw the ants feasting on corn and grain from the stores they had collected in the summer.

Then the grasshopper knew: it is best to prepare for days of need.

Answer the question by connecting the picture card.

Who was the story about?	
Where and when did it take place?	
What happened?	
What was the problem?	
How was it solved?	

Story Elements

Who was the story about?

characters: people or animals in the story

Where and when did it take place?

setting: time and place

What happened?

events: important things that happen in the story

What was the problem?

problem: troubling event or issue

How was it solved?

solution: event that solves the problem or ends story

Story Elements

Fill in the character and settings for Mia and David's favorite stories and then write about yours.

David's favorite character is Batman.
The story takes place in Gotham City.

Mia's favorite character is Ariel.
The story takes place under the sea.

	Character	Setting
David's		
Mia's		

Who are the character(s) and what is the setting for your favorite story?

_____

_____

_____

_____

The Tortoise and the Hare

The Hare was boasting of his speed before the other animals. "I have never been beaten!" he said. "When I run full speed, I challenge anyone here to race against me."

The Tortoise said quietly, "I accept your challenge."

"That is a good joke," said the Hare. "I could dance round you all the way."

"Shall we race?" answered the Tortoise.

So a course was fixed at the park and a start was made. **The Hare** darted almost out of sight at once, but soon stopped and, to show his contempt for the Tortoise, **lay down to have a nap.** The Tortoise plodded on, and when the Hare awoke from his nap, he saw the Tortoise just near the winning-post and could not catch up in time to save the race.

"Slow but steady wins the race," said the Tortoise.

What is the main problem in the story that explains why the hare lost the race?

_____

_____

_____

Match the story elements from the story *The Tortoise and the Hare.*

1	The race.	
2	The Hare took a nap.	
3	Slow but steady wins the race.	
4	The park.	
5	The Hare and the Tortoise.	

| Solution | Characters | Events | Setting | Problem |

Write a story outline for your own story.

GRAMMAR   SPELLING   **STORY ELEMENTS**

Title: _____

Characters: _____

Setting: _____

Event(s): _____

Problem: _____

Solution: _____

Name_____

Story Elements Quiz

1. A solution is an event that solves a problem in a story. True or false?

2. What is the setting in **The Tortoise and the Hare**?
   a. Hare
   b. race
   c. park
   d. nap

3. What is the problem in one of the stories that you read?
   a. The Ant collected food for the winter.
   b. The Hare took a nap.
   c. The Tortoise took his time in the race.
   d. The Grasshopper learned a lesson.

4. What is the main character in one of the stories that you read?
   a. nap
   b. food
   c. Ant
   d. worry

5. Which is the solution in one of the stories that you read?
   a. The Grasshopper was hungry.
   b. The tortoise on because he didn't stop.
   c. The Grasshopper did not want to work.
   d. The Hare took a nap during the race.

Narrative Point of View

Key Vocabulary

narrator

point of view

first person

second person

Third person limited

Third person omniscient

Perspective

Read the passages below and consider the narrative point of view.

first person — **I**

I realized I would have to act quickly if I was going to save my brother.

second person — **You**

You walk out on stage, your stomach is in knots, the lights are hot and everyone is looking at you.

third person — **He**

It was a dream come true. He had always wanted to visit his uncle in Africa and his parents had finally agreed.

The narrative point of view is the perspective from which tfirsthe story is told. We use the terms first-, second-, or third-person to describe the narrative point of view.

First, Second or Third Person.

Read the passage and mark it 1st, 2nd or 3rd person.

Summary

1st   ☐   From the kitchen cupboard you gather the sugar, flour, and other ingredients that you need. You think to yourself how good your father's birthday cake will come out.

2nd   ☐   I woke up that morning and had a funny feeling that something unusual was going to happen and boy was I right.

3rd   ☐   When he was a little boy he had always wanted to grow up to be an astronaut.

---

1   First-person narrative

Narrator is a character in the story, and the story is told from that character's perspective using first-person pronouns such as *I* and we.

2   Second-person narrative

You, the reader, are the point of view. Not often used in fiction, but frequently used in songs, letters, poems and greeting cards.

3   Third-person narrative

Most common narrative form, as it allows the author to give the reader access to the thoughts and motivation of one or more characters in the story.

Change the story told by Tori in the first-person narrative mode to the third-person narrative mode.

The growling sound in the cave grew louder. **I** looked across at Fernando and said, "Let's get out of here now!"

We ran quickly to the cave entrance, but **I** slipped and fell awkwardly. "You go on without me," **I** said, clutching at **my** ankle. "I won't leave without you!" said Fernando bravely, as the growling sound echoed around the cave.

_____

The growling sound in the cave grew louder. _____ looked across at Fernando and said, "Let's get out of here now!"

_____ ran quickly to the cave entrance, but _____ slipped and fell awkwardly. "You go on without me," _____ said, clutching at _____ ankle. "I won't leave without you!" said Fernando bravely, as the growling sound echoed around the cave.

| she | Tori | They | her | Tori |

The difference between a limited and an omniscient third-person narrative

limited narrator

A sound from deep within the cave made Tori feel very nervous. From his expression, she sensed that Fernando felt the same way. She knew they could not stay there!

omniscient narrator

A sound from deep within the cave made Tori feel very nervous. Fernando felt the same way, but didn't want Tori to know he was afraid. They both secretly wanted to leave the cave.

A limited narrator tells a story from the point of view of only one character. An omniscient narrator tells the story from the points of view of multiple characters and shares their thoughts with us.

Name_____

Narrative Point of View Quiz

1. In the first-person point of view, we use the pronouns I, we and my. True or false?

2. You, the reader, are the point of view within second-person narratives. True or false?

3. A limited narrator tells the story of all the characters in a story. True or false?

4. Which word in the following sentence helps the reader determine the narrative mode? Maxine took a picture of the Golden Gate Bridge.
   a. Maxine
   b. picture
   c. Golden
   d. bridge

5. From what perspective does the third-person omniscient tell the story?

   _____
   _____

Author's Purpose

Key Vocabulary

author's purpose

entertain

inform

persuade

Author's Purpose

> An *author's purpose* is the main reason the author has for writing the piece. An author's purpose is usually to inform, to persuade, or to entertain.

What is the author's purpose of this news article? _____

MONDAY, JULY 20   US $2.50

The Mayfair Herald

Miracle Cure! Zamophin

Recommended dosage: 12 pills daily.

NEW FORMULA!

Cures baldness and varicose veins!

*May cause illness and death.

New drug's claims questioned.

Scientists dispute "bogus" Zamophin claims

Leading scientists have expressed skepticism about some of the claims made about the new so-called "wonder drug," Zamophin. According to the drug's manufacturers, Phyzodone Pharmaceuticals, Zamophin cures baldness, reduces cholesterol, and also alleviates varicose veins. However, scientists say that there is no evidence that the drug does any one of these things.

Continued on Page 3

Label the author's purpose for each sentence.

The Tyrannosaurus Rex could grow up to 15 feet tall, 40 feet long, and weigh 5 to 7 tons. ◯

Every street should be lined with trees; they look very nice and provide shade in the summer. ◯

The Battle of the Little Bighorn (also known as Custer's Last Stand) took place in 1876. ◯

Game night was hilarious. Dad knocked over his soda when got a correct answer! ◯

The Amazon River is located in Brazil and is over 120 miles long; slightly shorter than the Nile. ◯

Persuade   **I**nform   **E**ntertain

The author uses bright colors and interesting fonts to entertain the reader but is that the purpose of the advertisement? What do you think? Label the advertisement according to the author's purpose.

SLURPY SODA!
Real FRUIT JUICE gives you lots of energy, and the FIZZY BUBBLES make you popular! Try our delicious new TANGERINE flavor! ◯

Persuade   **I**nform   **E**ntertain

Author's Purpose

Although there is information in this poster, is the author's purpose to inform? What do you think. Label the poster according to the author's purpose.

9,500 lives were saved this year because of seatbelts.

Seat belts increase your chance of surviving a crash by 50%. 3 out of 4 crashes occur within 25 miles of home, so no matter how short the drive, buckle up!

P ersuade   **I** nform   **E** ntertain

What is the author's purpose in this passage?

The Tell Tale Heart by Edgar Allan Poe

It is impossible to say how first the idea entered my brain; but once conceived, it haunted me day and night. Object there was none. Passion there was none. I loved the old man. He had never wronged me. He had never given me insult. For his gold I had no desire. I think it was his eye! Yes, it was this! He had the eye of a vulture—a pale blue eye, with a film over it. Whenever it fell upon me, my blood ran cold; and so by degrees—very gradually—I made up my mind to take the life of the old man, and thus rid myself of the eye forever.

(**P**)ersuade   (**I**)nform   (**E**)ntertain

What is the authors' purpose in each of these articles?

"Baker's Dozen" is the Must See Show of the Year!	Fiction Series Pt III: The boy and the cottage	Debbi Jones is the New Mayor of Mayfair!
Everyone should see this show! You will be completely stunned by the brilliant portrayal of a classic hero! It will leave you hungry for more.	The boy, tattered and tired from his hike over the mountain, stumbled upon an old stone fence. He looked up to see a dilapidated cottage in the distance.	Debbi Jones celebrated her big win yesterday in the mayoral election. She soundly defeated the challenger, John Smith, by 500 votes.

inform	persuade	entertain

www.onboardacademics.com

Sort the types of writing by the author's purpose.

inform	entertain	persuade

poem   editorial   novel

billboard   biography   textbook

Name_____

Author's purpose Quiz

1. All parts of a newspaper are written to inform. True or false?

2. Which of the following is written to persuade?
   a. advertisements
   b. newspapers
   c. editorials
   d. both a and c

3. Which of the following are mostly meant to entertain?
   a. novels
   b. magazines
   c. comics
   d. all of the above

4. Which of the following are mostly meant to inform?
   a. poem
   b. billboard
   c. textbook
   d. all of the above

5. Text can be both informative and persuasive. True or false?

Literary Elements of Fiction

Key Vocabulary

setting

plot

character

problem

solution

Three Billy Goats Gruff

Once upon a time there were three billy goats, who were to go up to the hillside to make themselves fat, and the name of all three was "Gruff." On the way up was a bridge over a cascading stream they had to cross; and under the bridge lived a great ugly troll , with eyes as big as saucers, and a nose as long as a poker.

So first of all came the youngest Billy Goat Gruff to cross the bridge."Trip, trap, trip, trap! " went the bridge. "Who's that tripping over my bridge?" roared the troll . "Oh, it is only I, the tiniest Billy Goat Gruff , and I'm going up to the hillside to make myself fat," said the billy goat, with such a small voice. "Now, I'm coming to gobble you up," said the troll. "Oh, no! pray don't take me. I'm too little, that I am," said the billy goat. "Wait a bit till the second Billy Goat Gruff comes. He's much bigger." "Well, be off with you," said the troll.

A little while after came the second Billy Goat Gruff to cross the bridge. Trip, trap, trip, trap, trip, trap, went the bridge. "Who's that tripping over my bridge?" roared the troll. "Oh, it's the second Billy Goat Gruff , and I'm going up to the hillside to make myself fat," said the billy goat, who hadn't such a small voice. "Now I'm coming to gobble you up," said the troll. "Oh, no! Don't take me. Wait a little till the big Billy Goat Gruff comes. He's much bigger." "Very well! Be off with you," said the troll.

But just then up came the big Billy Goat Gruff . Trip, trap, trip, trap, trip, trap! went the bridge, for the billy goat was so heavy that the bridge creaked and groaned under him. "Who's that tramping over my bridge?" roared the troll. "It's I! The big Billy Goat Gruff ," said the billy goat, who had an ugly hoarse voice of his own. "Now I 'm coming to gobble you up," roared the troll.

Well, come along! I've got two spears,
And I'll poke your eyeballs out at your ears;
I've got besides two curling-stones,
And I'll crush you to bits, body and bones.

That was what the big billy goat said. And then he flew at the troll, and poked his eyes out with his horns, and crushed him to bits, body and bones, and tossed him out into the cascade, and after that he went up to the hillside. There the billy goats got so fat they were scarcely able to walk home again. And if the fat hasn't fallen off them, why, they're still fat; and so,

Snip, snap, snout.
This tale's told out.

Setting, Characters, Plot and Resolution

Setting

Characters

Plot

Resolution

- The **setting** is the location in which the story takes place.
- The **characters** are the people or creatures in the story. Sometime the main character is referred to as the protagonist.
- The **plot** describes the main conflict or problem in the story.
- The **resolution** of the plot means how does the protagonist(s) solve the problem or conflict.

Describe the setting in the story.

_____
_____
_____
_____
_____
_____
_____
_____
_____
_____
_____

Characters

 +

Describe the characters in the story.

_____
_____
_____
_____
_____
_____

Describe the plot in the story.

 want

but  wants

_____
_____
_____
_____
_____
_____
_____
_____
_____
_____

Resolution

Describe the resolution of *Three Billy Goats Gruff.*

Describe the plot in the story.

_____
_____
_____
_____
_____
_____
_____
_____
_____
_____
_____
_____

The Wolf in Sheep's Clothing — Aesop's Fables

A wolf found great difficulty in getting at the sheep owing to the vigilance of the shepherd and his dogs. But one day it found the skin of a sheep that had been flayed and thrown aside, so it put it on over its own pelt and strolled down among the sheep.

The lamb that belonged to the sheep, whose skin the wolf was wearing, began to follow the wolf in the sheep's clothing; so, leading the lamb a little apart, he soon made a meal off her, and for some time he succeeded in deceiving the sheep, and enjoying hearty meals.

What is the setting for the story?

Who is the main protagonist?

Explain the plot?

What is the theme of the story?
The theme is the central idea or moral of the story.

Animal Farm by George Orwell

Upset by conditions of neglect and cruelty at Manor Farm, the animals stage a revolution and eject the farmer and his men. Two pigs, Snowball and Napoleon, show great skill and leadership in the battle.

Now in control of the farm, the animals declare that "all animals are equal" and they meet regularly to discuss and agree farm policy. However, after a period of time, the **pigs** become the supervisors of the farm because of their superior intelligence.

With the help of a pack of vicious dogs that he has been rearing in secret, the power-hungry Napoleon eventually assumes total control of the farm and drives Snowball into exile. From this point, whenever things go wrong, Napoleon persuades the other animals that it is all Snowball's fault.

Over time, under Napoleon's command, the animal's society becomes less and less equal until the pigs begin to talk and act just like their former human masters.

What is the setting for the novel?

Who are the main protagonists?

Explain the plot?

What is the resolution of the novel?

What is the theme of the novel?

Animal Farm by George Orwell

What is the setting for the novel?
Manor Farm.

Who are the main protagonists?
The two pigs, Napoleon and Snowball.

Explain the plot?
The animals take over a farm with the intention of creating a just and equal society.

What is the resolution of the novel?
There is no positive resolution. The pigs abuse their power and act like their former human masters.

What is the theme of the novel?
Power corrupts. Can you explain this theme?

Name_____

Literary Elements of Fiction Quiz

1. The theme of a book is the lesson that the character learns. True or false?

2. I love the smell of the salty air and th sound of the waves breaking against the rocks. I can see the rising sun reflecting off the waves. What is the setting for this passage?_____

3. In *Animal Farm*, what problems to the animals have at the beginning of the novel?
   a. Conditions on the farm are harsh
   b. The pigs are power-hungry
   c. Napoleon and Snowball can't agree
   d. All animals are equal

4. Which literary element explains the main events of a fictional story?
   a. Protagonist
   b. plot
   c. resolution
   d. theme

5. Who is the protagonist in *Wolf in Sheep's Clothing*?

_____

Main Idea

Key Vocabulary

main idea

The Main Idea

> **Thinking about an appropriate title for a passage can help you to find the main idea. The main idea is the overall idea of a passage; the main point or message that the passage conveys.**

Read the passage and think of a title. Enter it in the box.

In order to keep pets such as cats and small dogs safe from coyotes, do not leave them unsupervised outside for long periods of time, especially at dusk or early in the morning. Build a fence to keep coyotes out of your yard, making sure that the fence is partially submerged under the ground, and don't leave food outside since this may attract coyotes to your property. Outside cats are very vulnerable, and so for her safety, consider making Tiddles an "indoor cat". When walking a dog, keep it leashed to reduce the likelihood of a coyote encounter.

Identify the main idea in this paragraph.

Jenna is planning to compete in a triathlon. She has been training for nearly three months and her schedule consists of swimming, cycling and running: the three elements of a triathlon. She is being very careful with her diet, and is eating lots of fruit and pasta, and drinking plenty of fluids. Last week, she purchased a new bike especially for the event. The bike cost over $400, but her parents have said they will contribute half the cost if Jenna finishes in the top 10 for her age group.

○　Jenna is planning to compete in a triathlon

○　There are three elements in a triathlon

○　Jenna has been training for nearly three months

Find the main idea and supporting details.
Write the main idea in the blue box and supporting details in the white boxes.

☐ Main idea　☐ Supporting details

• Many parents prefer to drive their children to school.
• Ridership of school busses is decreasing.
• Students who live close enough prefer to walk to school.
• Sneakers are quite expensive.
• Students think the bus leaves too early.

Circle the main idea. Underline the supporting details and draw a line through text that doesn't support the main idea.

I wish I had a robot as my personal servant. The robot would do all of my homework, tidy my room, and clean my teeth. I would even command it to eat my broccoli when my mom wasn't looking. I could hire my robot out to neighbors in order to make extra money.

My robot would wash cars, cut lawns, and walk dogs... all for a very reasonable price. I think "Mr. Brains" would be a good name for my robot.

Suggest a title for this passage that identifies the main idea.

Title

There are several main differences between alligators and crocodiles. If you get up close to a crocodile (and we wouldn't recommend it!), then you'll notice that when its mouth is closed, one of its lower teeth sticks up over its upper lip. You'll also notice that the crocodile's snout is v-shaped. Alligators have rounder more u-shaped snouts. Habitat is another way to distinguish between a crocodile and an alligator. Alligators typically live in freshwater, while crocodiles live in both freshwater and saltwater habitats.

Can you summarize the main idea and the supporting details in a single sentence?

Name_____

Main Idea Quiz

1. The main idea identifies what paragraph or a passage is mostly about. True or false?

2. Which sentence supports the main idea that apples are good for your health?
   a. Apples are a good source of fiber which aids in digestion
   b. Apples can be sliced and made into pie.
   c. My grandfather took us apple picking in October
   d. Apples cost more out of season.

3. Which sentence supports the mian idea that you should wear a seatbelt?
   a. Cars usually have 4-7 seatbelts.
   b. Make sure the seatbelt is secure
   c. Seatbelts keep people safely in thier seats.
   d. Seatbelts look similar.

4. What is the most important function of supporting details?
   a. They tell us important information.
   b. The support the main idea.
   c. They wrap up a sentence.
   d. They are interesting.

Topic

Key Vocabulary

broad

relate

Topic

The topic is the broad, general subject matter of a passage.

What is the topic of this paragraph. Select from the three suggestions below.

It's hard to imagine daily life without electronic gadgets. We stay connected with friends and family with laptops and cell phones. We listen to an mp3 player while going for a walk or waiting for the bus. And many people end their day relaxing in front of the TV or watching a DVD.

Topic	

Daily life

Electronic gadgets

It's hard to imagine daily life without electronic gadgets

Topics Unite

> ## The topic *unites* related ideas or items.

_____

Select the topic that unites these words and phrases from the three suggestions given.

traffic jam
sirens
flashing lights
ambulance
mangled car
crowd of people

leaving work car accident movie shoot

Organize by Topic

Organize the words by topic.

painting	yard work	bicycle

exercise	work gloves	brake	easel
gear	lawnmower	helmet	shears
creativity	leaves	canvas	brushes

The Topic and The Main Idea

Read the passage below and then review the topic and the main idea.

Red roses are an enduring symbol of love. In early cultures, wedding ceremonies would be decorated with red roses. The rose can be found in mythology as the symbol for Aphrodite the goddess of love. Throughout history countless poets and artists have used the red rose as a symbol of love. Today the red rose is used to celebrate Valentines Day.

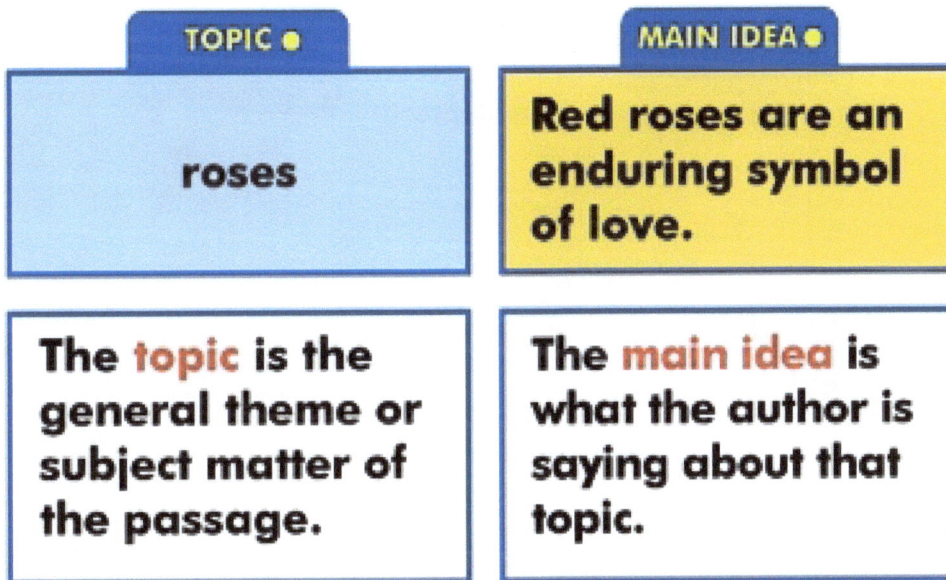

TOPIC ●

roses

MAIN IDEA ●

Red roses are an enduring symbol of love.

The topic is the general theme or subject matter of the passage.

The main idea is what the author is saying about that topic.

Identify the topic and the main idea of the following paragraph.

Sarah had a birthday party yesterday. Her mom had spent all morning baking a beautiful birthday cake. Sarah was up at seven cleaning the house. Then, she decorated the whole house with balloons that she had tied to chairs and streamers hanging from the walls. In the afternoon Sarah's mom ran out to the store to pick up some last minute party favors. When the guests had finally arrived Sarah and her mom were a little tired from all the preparation.

topic	
main idea	

Sarah hates her birthday.   Sarah's birthday party

Hosting a party is hard work.   decorating

Doing chores takes time.   cleaning the house

More Topic and Main Idea Identification

Identify the topic and the main idea of the paragraph below.

It is a long road to becoming a surgeon. After four years of college, students who gain entry to medical school will then have four years of further study. Medical school graduates then need to intern for a year, which means learning in a real-world environment. Finally, there is a surgical residency, where aspiring surgeons work in hospitals and participate in surgeries. This can take from 2-8 years!

topic	
main idea	

The Topic Sentence

> The topic sentence is a single sentence
> that expresses the author's main idea.

_____

Underline the topic sentence.

It is a long road to becoming a surgeon. After four years of college, students who gain entry to medical school will then have four years of further study. Medical school graduates then need to intern for a year, which means learning in a real-world environment. Finally, there is a surgical residency, where aspiring surgeons work in hospitals and participate in surgeries. This can take from 2-8 years!

Name_____

Topic Quiz

1. Most information in a passage relates back to the topic.
   True or false?

2. Which statement best defines the term topic?
   a. a summary of a passage
   b. supporting details in a passage
   c. the main idea of a passage
   d. the general theme of a passage

3. What is the difference between the topic and the main
   idea of a passage?
   a. The main idea provides information about the topic.
   b. The topic provides information about the main idea.
   c. They are broadly the same thing.
   d. The topic provides the author's viewpoint.

4. Which topic word is most closely related to the
   following words? roast, strain, broil
   a. farm
   b. eat
   c. cook
   d. clean

Supporting Details

Key Vocabulary

topic

main idea

supporting details

The Main Idea

> The **main idea** is the *key concept* being
> expressed. The **supporting details** describe
> the main idea; they *support* the main idea.

Which of the sentences below support the main idea? Add any of the sentences
below that are supporting detail.

☐ main idea   ☐ supporting detail

Black Labradors are friendly pets.
Labs naturally have a sweet and gentle disposition.
They will sit by the door, anticipating your return.

Labs excitedly jump and bark when you return home.

They are born in a litter of puppies.

Labs are protective and growl at unfamiliar people.

They always wag their tail when they see you.

     www.onboardacademics.com

Supporting details are often facts, opinions and descriptions.

Label the supporting detail as fact, opinion or description.

Coral snakes are deadly animals.	
Coral snakes have alternating black, red and yellow bands	
They are highly venomous. Their venom causes paralysis	
This is why they are the world's most feared snakes	

fact	opinion	description

Re-order the supporting detail in sequential order.

> Supporting details are usually presented in **sequential order** (the order in which they happen). This helps to develop and clarify the main idea.

> Look for **signal words** to help you to order the events.

1	Pack the equipment and snacks in a lightweight bag (making sure to include the map).
2	Lastly, bring a friend to make the hike safer and more enjoyable.
3	Before you start packing, make sure you have enough food and water for your hike.
4	First, you need to purchase the appropriate equipment, like sturdy boots and water bottles.
5	Then decide on the trail you want to hike and make sure you have a detailed map.

1	
2	
3	
4	
5	

Add supporting details to the main idea.

> # Main ideas rely on *supporting details* the same way that a chair seat relies on the legs.

Chairs are a household necessity.

They are needed if you want to sit at a table to eat.

Supporting detail relates to the main idea.

Label the supporting detail by which main idea it relates to by placing an E or an H in the corresponding box.

> (**E**) **Summer vacation *enhances* student performance.**
>
> (**H**) **Summer vacation *hinders* student performance.**

- ☐ Students can become depressed and lose motivation if they are never given the opportunity to relax and have fun.

- ☐ Students can very quickly lose good study habits.

- ☐ Other countries continually push their students to work harder and this gives them a competitive advantage.

- ☐ Summer vacation gives students time to pursue other interests which helps to expand their skills and experience.

- ☐ Students returning to school after a long break find it very difficult to concentrate.

- ☐ Summer vacation is like the off season for a football player. It's a time to relax and recharge your batteries.

Identify if the supporting detail is relevant to the main idea.

Mark it with a √ if its relevant or an X if it is not relevant.

There are many things to do at the beach.	
You can swim or just float in the water.	☐
Some people just like to sunbathe.	☐
Always wear at least 30 SPF sunscreen.	☐
Lifeguards have extensive training.	☐
Other people like to read at the beach.	☐

✓

✗

Use the supporting idea to find the main idea.

[   ] are a [   ] way to get [   ] in a [   ]. They are very convenient and allow large numbers of people to get to their destinations quickly and easily. It is relatively inexpensive to travel by subway, and taking the subway eliminates both the frustration and the cost of parking on congested city streets. Subways also help the city's environment as they generate much less pollution than cars.

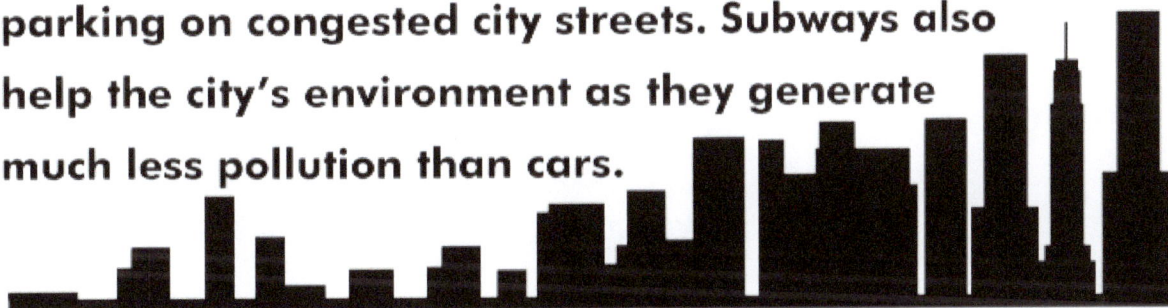

Name_____

Supporting Details Quiz

1. A main idea does not need supporting details. True or false?

2. Which of the following does not support the main idea that water is good for you?
   a. Water is now a very fashionable drink.
   b. Your body requires eight glasses of water per day.
   c. Water cleanses your system.
   d. Water helps you to feel more awake and alert.

3. The main idea is always the first sentence of a paragraph. True or false?

4. Which of the following would be considered a supporting detail?
   a. a fact
   b. an opinion
   c. an example
   d. all of the above

5. Which sentence is a supporting detail for the main idea that keeping animals in a zoo is cruel?
   a. Zoos play an important conservation role.
   b. Many zoo animals are rescue animals.
   c. Animals should be in their natural environment.
   d. Great improvements have been made to animal enclosures in zoos

Main Idea

Key Vocabulary

topic

main idea

topic sentence

detail sentence

www.onboardacademics.com

The Main Idea

The main idea is the most important idea that the paragraph conveys. It is also known as the main point or message of a paragraph.

What is the main idea of this paragraph? Place a check mark next to the main idea below.

There are many kinds of farms. Some farms have lots of different animals, while other farms have just one main animal like poultry, sheep, or horses. Many farms don't have any animals at all!

Cows and chickens live on a farm.

There are many kinds of farms.

You can find horses on a farm

The topic and main idea in a paragraph.

Read the passage below and note the difference between the main idea and the topic. Each is highlight to show the difference.

TOPIC ●

Digging a hole can be tough work. It is difficult to push the shovel into the hard dirt, and sometimes you have to remove large rocks by hand.

The **topic** is the general subject matter of the paragraph (what the paragraph is about).

MAIN IDEA ●

Digging a hole can be tough work. It is difficult to push the shovel into the hard dirt, and sometimes you have to remove large rocks by hand.

The **main idea** is the most important idea in a paragraph. It is the main point in the text.

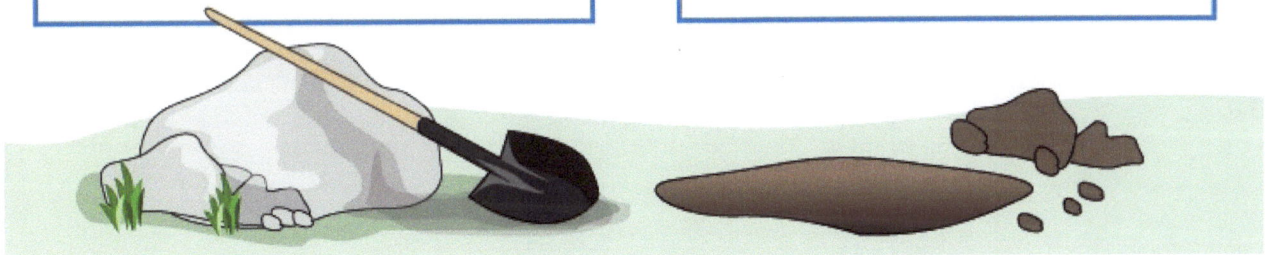

Identify the topic and the main idea.

Select from the options to identify both the topic and the main idea in the following paragraph.

Alison loves to play games. Her favorite game is chess because it requires a great deal of thought. Alison also likes to play board games that are based mostly on luck. When Alison is alone she likes to amuse herself with a game of *Solitaire*.

topic	main idea

how smart Alison is	Alison likes to think
playing games	Alison likes *Solitaire*
chess	Alison enjoys playing games

What is the main idea in each paragraph?

Mia organized a picnic at a park. She invited a group of her friends. Everyone brought one dish to share. They played different games, and walked around the park.

main idea

Computers have changed so much over the years. An early model could add 18 million numbers per hour. A modern computer can add 1.5 trillion numbers in three hours.

main idea

Topic Sentence and Detailed Sentence

TOPIC SENTENCE •

You should take great pride in your homework. First, make sure that you read all of the directions. Complete the work neatly. Be sure to check over your work before you are done, and turn it in on time.

The topic sentence expresses the *main idea* of the paragraph, and is usually the first sentence.

DETAIL SENTENCE •

You should take great pride in your homework. First, make sure that you read all of the directions. Complete the work neatly. Be sure to check over your work before you are done, and turn it in on time.

Detail sentences give more information about the main idea and support the topic sentence.

Select the missing topic sentence from the available options below.

Make sure that the bike is in working order. Check the brakes and test your light and horn. Purchase a helmet and knee pads and wear them while riding. Never carry people on your handlebars.

Always wear a helmet.

Riding a bike is fun.

Bike safety is important.

The main ingredients are usually fresh vegetables which have lots of important nutrients for the body. Generally, salads are low in calories and, apart from the dressing, contain very little sugar or fat.

Lettuce is in a salad.

Eating salads is healthy.

Salad dressing is good.

Identify if the sentences below are a topic sentence 'T' or a detail sentence 'D'.

1   **Starfish are amazing animals.**   ☐

2   **Dogs can be great helpers.**   ☐

3   **These dogs often lead blind people.**   ☐

4   **It's next to the park in the middle of the city.**   ☐

5   **First, you mix the milk with the chocolate.**   ☐

6   **Fixing a flat tire on a bicycle is easy.**   ☐

Unscramble the paragraphs below and underline the topic sentence.

Players also learn how to defend the hoop.

They learn how to dribble, pass, and shoot the ball.

Most importantly, they learn how to be team players.

Basketball players need to learn many different skills.

Finally, take the two pieces and press them together.

First, spread a scoop of peanut butter on a slice of bread.

Then take another slice of bread and spread jelly on it.

A peanut butter and jelly sandwich is very easy to make.

www.onboardacademics.com

Name_____

Main Idea Quiz

1. A detail sentence tells the main idea. True or false?

2. Put an X next to the sentences that tells the main idea.
   a. It's nice to help your brother get ready for bed.
   b. Make sure to give him a bath.
   c. Put on a clean pair of pajamas.
   d. Read him a story, and turn off the light.

3. Place an X next to the sentence that does not add to the main idea that baseball is a fun sport.
   a. You can play it with your friends.
   b. It's good to exercise.
   c. My knee hurts.
   d. The crowd will cheer you on.

4. Details are more specific than the main topic sentence. True or false?

5. Place an X next to the sentence that supports the main idea that teachers work hard.
   a. My teacher has blond hair.
   b. Our classroom is on the first floor.
   c. Our teacher always has new, fun lessons for us.
   d. We play games at recess.

Features of Non-fiction Text

Key Vocabulary

table of contents

heading

glossary

index

Non-Fiction Elements

| T | List of all of the chapters in a book and the page number on which the chapter starts. |

| I | Illustrations and photos that accompany the text |

| BI | The author uses this technique to draw my attention to these words or phrases |

| H | Title or caption that describes a paragraph or section of the book |

| G | Alphabetical list of special words with their definitions – usually found at the end of a book. |

| IN | Alphabetical list of key words and terms with all of the pages numbers on which they appear. |

Contents

Understanding Your Co
   The hard disk.................
   Memory.......................
   The monitor.................
   The power supply.........
Peripherals.....................
   Printers.......................
   Scanners....................
   External devices..........
   Backup........................
The Internet....................
   Browsers.....................
   Security.......................
   Web 2.0......................
   Social networking.........
Glossary.........................

| IN | Index | G | Glossary | BI | Bold _or italicized_ |
| T | Table of Contents | I | Images | H | Heading |

Table of Contents

Contents

Understanding Your Computer   Page 11
    The hard disk...................................12
    Memory...17
    The monitor.......................................33
    The power supply..............................37
Peripherals...**45**
    Printers..47
    Scanners..55
    External devices................................65
    Backup...75
The Internet..**77**
    Browsers..83
    Security..92
    Web 2.0..100
    Social networking..............................115
Glossary..**125**

1 If you wanted to learn about printers, which page would you go to?

2 Which subject is addressed on page 51?

3 On which page will I find definitions for computer parts and accessories?

Glossary

Glossary

Hard Drive
This is where documents, files and programs are stored on the computer.

RAM Memory
RAM or "random access memory" provides temporary data storage. All data in RAM is lost when the computer is switched off.

CPU
The CPU is the 'brain' of a computer responsible for processing all of the instructions.

USB Ports
Ports which enable devices such as mice and keyboards to be attached to the computer.

Power Supply
Provides electrical power to the computer.

I can store all of my photos and music here.

This is where I attach my music player to my computer.

This provides my computer with short-term storage.

Headings

Add the headings listed below to this London tour guide.

Great Stuff To See And Do When You Visit London

Bought in 1761 by George III, this Palace is the London residency for the Queen and boasts more than 350 different types of wildflowers!

Take a short train ride to this 300-acre botanical wonderland and see the world's largest plant in a beautiful setting by the river Thames.

Find out why the dinosaurs became extinct and have your picture taken with a 26-metre-long diplodocus at this world-famous museum.

Book ahead for a ride on the world's tallest observation wheel standing at about 450 ft high and providing fantastic views of London in all directions!

If you like hanging out with wax celebrities, then don't miss this attraction. You might run into Brad and Angelina if you're lucky!

At various times an armory, a palace, and a place of execution, remember to keep your head when you visit the famous Beefeaters at this popular attraction!

The London Eye **Natural History Museum** **The Tower of London**

Kew Gardens **Madame Tussaud's** **Buckingham Palace**

Bold or *Italicized* Words

Circle the parts of the text that should be **bold** or *italicized*.

Diplodocus

Diplodocus was a giant beast measuring 90 ft from head to tail and weighing in at 15 tons. A herbivore, *Diplodocus* lived about 150 million years ago. Its stomach was full of smooth pebbles that helped it to break down and digest food.

Diplodocus *dip-LOD-oh-kus*

Allosaurus

Although it was a huge and ferocious beast, measuring about 40 ft in length, Allosaurus did not have the jaw strength of a Tyrannosaurus, and so used its jagged teeth to bleed its prey.

Velociraptor

A small, but very athletic pack hunter, *Velociraptor* used a foot claw to inflict terrible wounds on its prey. You might remember Velociraptor from a scene in a famous movie, Jurassic Park.

Name_____

Features of Non-Fiction Text Quiz

1. The index of a non-fiction book lists the chapters and is usually found at the beginning. True or false?

2. The table of contents shows illustrations. True or false?

3. Which of the following is NOT true about the glossary?
   a. The glossary defines important words
   b. The glossary is in alphabetical order
   c. The glossary contains page numbers
   d. The glossary defines technical terms

4. What is the purpose of headings?
   a. To define important terms
   b. To interest the reader
   c. To explain the main idea of the paragraph
   d. To explain the pronunciation of words.

5. The table of contents is in alphabetical order. True or false?

6. Why are words in non-fiction texts sometimes bold or italicized? _____

_____

_____